$1200 and a Dream

An Entrepreneur's Guide

David Ecker

This publication is a nonfiction book designed with information from our experience but not produced to represent any person. The publication showcases how a concept can be accomplished via covered subject matter. We have placed information in this book that has worked for us but others may experience different results.

Library of Congress Control Number: 2023900306
ISBN Number: 979-8-9869637-2-3

Acknowledgments

I have to start by thanking my fabulous/brilliant wife, Allison. Her support in brainstorming, reading drafts, and advice made this all possible. I would be amiss if I didn't thank my son, Joshua, for always giving me his thoughts. Without them, this wouldn't have been possible.

Thank you to all the students I have worked with over the years who have challenged me.

David Ecker

Table of Contents

Introduction 7

Networking 11

Failure 21

Overcome Change 37

Risk 43

Generating Ideas 53

Foundation 59

Customer Perspective 71

Marketing 79

Presentations 92

Steps to become an Entrepreneur 106

Additional Resources 110

About the author 112

Introduction

This book is the foundation of how everyday people turn into entrepreneurs. Entrepreneurs have passion and drive that leads them to greatness. You have that ability. I believe that everyone can achieve this status in life.

This book is set up to offer you skills, exercises, and information that will help you move forward with your ideas.

To ensure we can get you to be an entrepreneur in the workplace or your own business. There are practical skills that you require to meet your objectives. Since we focus on the practical side, we aren't going to go into depth—the aim is to use this as a guide to the skills necessary. Once you have these skills, we will test your idea with customers.

Nothing is straightforward in life, but it's all doable; the skills that education teaches sometimes go to much into theoretical concepts, which misses the natural trouble spots that some of us need to overcome our worries.

I started a university campus maker/innovation space at Stony Brook University with a single facility, a 30-year-old Physics lab, $1200, and a dream. I knew it was possible to give students on campus a way to have hands-on learning to grow the knowledge they learned in the classroom into practical ideas. Given them, this learning was key to them being entrepreneurial in their life. We achieved this over time, growing to have helped at least five startup businesses, six innovation-oriented facilities, pitch competitions, partnerships with donors/alumni/companies, academic departments, and student organizations. We had over twenty thousand students utilize our services.

The foundation we built in this facility was ideal when COVID-19 hit New York. We didn't have enough PPE (Personal Protective Equipment) for first responders or hospital workers. We used our 3D printers and knowledge to design & produce Face Shields. We shared our designs with local libraries that put together an army of 3D printers to help our community. We shared our concept with others nationwide, and they began making similar designs throughout different libraries, homes, and maker spaces worldwide. We made a difference by helping the first-line responders with their needs so they could protect us.

Anything is possible with $1200 and a Dream.

How to use this book:

I designed this book as an interactive guide to help you develop the critical elements in your journey to start a new company. I will cover each concept separately to help us understand and implement them to focus on your goals. As a practical guide, this has examples to illustrate concepts. It is not designed to go into immense detail; other books cover details. Our focus is on getting you to understand your entrepreneurial level and how to implement your first venture.

This book has several prompts that ask the reader a question and leave space for them to write their answer. This is designed to help the reader think about the concept and examples given. It is best to complete the answer immediately after reading the previous few paragraphs.

Note: All answers are correct with these questions. These questions are designed to help you think and make you address things that you see need to be improved. By seeing the improvements, you can format a solution that would be the foundation of any company.

The first few chapters are designed to have you explore your ability to be an entrepreneur from networking, failure, and risk.

The second set of chapters is specifically designed to help you on your journey to be an entrepreneur, from generating ideas to marketing and presentations.

If you have suggestions, please drop me a note:
Email: davidicreate@gmail.com

Networking

A core skill that Entrepreneurs need to possess is the ability to engage and talk with colleagues, partners, and future customers. Networking is the ability to interact by building a group of contacts and colleagues in your sphere. This group may consist of colleagues, classmates, friends, and other entrepreneurs with whom you will interact over your life. They are the ones that you can count on that will work with when projects arise or when you have ideas that can provide value to them across your company or various outside organizations. Associating with various people in your life will give you a diverse group that can challenge, mentor, and pushes you through those difficult times that all entrepreneurs encounter during their journey.

Networking is the ability to interface with multiple people across various industries and keep updated with their careers and lives. As part of this skill, you need to be able to work with people at all levels of organizations, from high-level CEOs to technical experts. Great people know how to talk to everyone no matter their level and can make them feel comfortable.

This ability to network with a larger variety of people will allow all entrepreneurs to succeed in any opportunity. Networking is guided by the ability to interface and find a specific idea that will be reasonable with each person in a way that will allow them to build a shared connection among the individuals.

In-person networking is done through 1:1 conversation. Group or party networking is different since it may involve shorter conversations with many people around the room.

What first words come to mind when you think of networking?

These skills you need to learn how effectively improve your interactions with people:

1. Ability to introduce yourself to strangers:

   a) You might think this is easy, but one of the most complex parts any entrepreneur must face is the difficulty they will fail when they try to meet someone.
   b) Having something to say. When you introduce yourself, you need to open up the conversation with whom you are without interrupting.
   c) Everyday things to bring up are: hobbies, sports, travel, clothing, and careers

2. Active Listening to hear what the stranger is saying:

How do I actively listen? You must be able to interface with people; when you arrive, the focus must be on this new stranger. Phones and other distractions need to be ignored.

   a) Active Listening is the ability to focus on the person and hear what they are saying without responding immediately. When you respond, you ask a question about what they just spoke to you about, don't bring up anything with you, and focus on the person you are with. By doing this, you are engaging them and demonstrating that in this situation or in any future, you will listen to the investments from this corporation.

   b) Most people find asking a question about them related to their business, career, or family. These are great ways to start a conversation; if those don't work, find something that is a shared experience, like why you are both attending this event. Finding something to talk about will allow you to have a friendly conversation, and you can focus on active listening.

   c) You would like to keep track of this when you reach out in the future. You can remember so specific about that person.

Whatis the hardest part of active listening?

3. Eye contact:

This is the ability to look someone in the eye and ask a question. Eye contact allows people to see you as an individual who can care for and understand their point of view. It's this ability that opens us to future collaborations. I knew someone who had difficulty with this, but after working on it for a while, he found the conversations he had were more profound than before he could make eye contact.

4. Getting to know people:

a) People like it when you know them more than just what they do for a job. People like to be social. To stand out, you must find an activity you can do: a volunteer opportunity, a charity, or some other aspect of life with a shared interest.

b) This shared interest in ideas is the key you will use to keep connected with this person. Having shared interests will develop your relationship, which is the goal. You would like this person to become your friend.

5. Spending time with them:

a) After this initial encounter, find a time to meet with them on the phone or in person, where you can connect with them to follow up on their interests. This is not an opportunity to sell them on anything. You want to connect and follow up. This is usually one or two weeks after your initial meeting.

b) Some people like to exercise together, while others like to go to the bar or have a meal together.

c) This concept is where you give up your time and want to be with another person. Our time is valuable, so how we choose to spend it is noticed by other.

6. How do you start a conversation or initially contact someone new?

It would be best if you made that connection in the initial meeting; this is the best way to build something. Exchanging phone information, email, and social media or connecting with them via LinkedIn.

a) Ideas on how to connect:
Through a joint friend. If you know someone who knows the person, you can ask them for an introduction email similar to this.

Hi Chris.

I wanted to introduce you to Sally; you might have met her at the Spring party at my house a few weeks ago. I thought the two of you could help each other with your businesses.

Sally is a design consultant and may be able to help with the design of that room you and your wife were thinking of changing.

Chris is a construction manager, and his wife wants to change their family room into a more split game room and movie house.

Talk to you soon

b) A blind email works:

Hi Chris,

This is Dave from the Spring party earlier this week; it was great hearing about how your rocket technology is progressing toward moving satellites to space. I was hoping we could connect to hear more about this technology and if I could lend a hand.

Looking forward to hearing from you soon

Your Name

Offering to help get people interested as well as talking about their business and focus shows you were listening to the conversation and willing to continue it. People like to talk about what interests them.

8. Staying connected with your friends and colleagues:

a) This is the area in which most people fail because it takes a lot of work and patience. It's keeping in touch with them regularly. The friend/colleague you speak with once a year isn't going to be as developed or give you advice as the one you talk with multiple times a year. This is crucial as one of the significant parts that make entrepreneurs successful.

b) You must keep in touch with them at least every 4-6 weeks. It's essential if you want to stay updated.

People ask why so frequently. This is the optimal time for things to occur, but you to still stay updated on their journeys. This is vital as you want their help as you promote your new venture to a broader audience.

9. Methods for staying connected:

  a) Via a group email you cc people to keep them updated on what is going on with your business. Always ask them for advice; the ones that reply you know are interested in staying connected. I use this technique when I need to keep updated with a group of 30 or more people.

  b) Post on social media, LinkedIn is my preferred area where several colleagues are connected. When you post, tag them in the post. This allows them to be engaged with the comment that you mentioned.

  c) Sending them an individual email that talks about their interests.

  d) Calling them on the phone (this is something most people don't do, but it gives it a letter of a personal touch). I find this method to be the most valuable since it takes time, and you can understand other person's ideas and listen to feedback cooperatively.

10. How do you stay organized with information?

  a) This is the aspect that drives all of the networking. Keeping track of information about each person you talk to regularly.

  b) Companies are known to use complex people management systems that include tags, interactions, and notes. This ensures each person who interfaces with a client has all the information at their fingertips. They keep information such as when their last call occurred, favorite color, names of family members, and home address. This is a contact management system. (CMS). Or also called Contact Relationship Management System (CRMS)

  c) Individuals have different techniques:

- Keep it all in their heads and can bring it out from memory. I read that former US president Bill Clinton could remember every person he had ever met, and when he ran into them again, he could recall their name quickly.

- Use a calendar where they mark or schedule calls with colleagues.

- Writing them down in a book with pen and paper.

- Utilize Google Docs or Office 365 to track conversations.

A friend taught me that they use a method where they take a quick note about each interaction; there is no need to detail, just a few facts or points discussed. This helps them recall the conversation and flow with any follow-up conversation needed.

11. Action items:

An action item is a task that you will need to complete after the conversation. It's a way of ensuring that you complete the item.

a) Most people need to write down in some form to remember what they want to do after the calls. Electronic means have become the preferred method after the pandemic (COVID-19)

b) Currently, there are card-based systems such as Trello and/or ClickUp. Put a card for each interaction, and you can move it from a column that needs action or a completed area.

c) Most phones now have apps such as PostIt notes and/or Tasks that remind them when something needs to be completed.

d) Larger systems such as OneNote or Evernote are robust note systems, but people find methods where they tag, folders, and annotations that allow them to have a workflow.

e) Any method that works for you is the most efficient.

I find a board-based system like Trello/Click Up efficient because it allows you to organize little sticky notes based on a higher-level category. I use this for colleagues, business partners, family, and friends. This ensures I can prioritize one category over another. These systems also allow for due dates, which is essential if research needs to be done and feedback is given.

In addition, I find Evernote to be a large-scale note, email, document, and electronic repository that would allow you to keep information more than just follow-up conversations.

Networking has numerous ways to achieve results, but it should be efficient and collaborative. If you don't want to build a network, be honest with yourself and don't waste others' time.

I have learned that some people want to utilize you for your knowledge without reciprocating in any way. I'm afraid that's not right and will only waste people's time, resulting in a negative outlook that is not anyone desired result.

Generally, people who want to connect are looking for a long relationship, and that's what networking is at its core. It's connecting with people for mutual gain or respect.

W hat is your preferred method of keeping track of networking interactions? If you don't have one, what system are you going to try?

Here are links to the systems and applications mentioned in this area:

- Trello – https://www.trello.com
- Clickup - https://clickup.com
- Google Keep Notes – https://keep.google.com/
- Apple Reminders - https://www.icloud.com/reminders
- Evernote – https://evernote.com/
- OneNote – https://www.onenote.com/

David Ecker

Failure

Failure is something that we all encounter in our lives. It's the people that stand up to this failure and can overcome it will be the ones that can achieve

Failure is something I have found to be empowering throughout my career. We can see things as they are, but things never go straightforwardly. There was an instance when I was working with the engineering department, and they didn't feel that a facility was being used by enough students. Even though a previous colleague indicated, this was a more open collaboration space used by students than the heavy machining labs they had in the past. I brought up the benefits this facility could bring to community, but the engineering leadership had a different viewpoint. They saw it as a facility that could be used for other purposes. I see this as my inability to convince the leadership the value of this facility, as a failure to help bring hands-on learning to that area. I knew it was the right objective for students and the campus community to have this facility in that department to learn through hands-on learning, but it was out of my control. It took over six months to redistribute the technology installed in the facility and they modified the facility to serve a different objective.

This was a failure to convince the engineering department that this facility had specific value toward engineering students. In the end the students lost since there wasn't an equivalent replacement in the engineering area. Most people see this failure as a stain that won't come off their clothes. But I am always empowered by failure and believe in the ability to fail forward. It's not easy, but it's the life we all have to weather in any career.

When encountering this, we must decide our next steps and how we will learn and grow from this experience. We can't just get frustrated and sulking; some things cause people to spiral and never feel like they can take the next steps.

We should all follow the FAIL approach, which stands for Failure, Approach, Improvement, and Learning. Using the FAIL method, we cannot only overcome but turn each failure into something that helps us achieve more than when the incident occurred.

1. Failure - What happened?
2. Approach - Why did it occur?
3. Improvements - What improvements can you make?
4. Learn - What did you learn from all this?

Step 1 Failure:

We all encounter failure in relationships, school, jobs, business, and life. If we don't have an opportunity to fail and have difficulties, we can grow to become better people. It takes a lot for us to understand that this is humbling and difficult when it occurs.

Can you think of a failure that occurred to you? (Write down the failure in a few sentences here)

How did you feel? Good? Bad? Let down? Sad? Frustrated? (Write down your feelings)

All of these are normal feelings, and we wouldn't be human if we didn't feel this way. Now we need to understand what occurred.

Think about the failure. Why did it occur? Spirit Airlines agreed to merge with Frontier Airlines to merge low-cost carriers. But during the process, JetBlue decided it would be better to merge with Spirit. JetBlue offered more money and gave Spirit additional reasons that made them rethink which direction they wanted to take the company. Eventually, Spirit decided to go with JetBlue. Frontier Airlines failed to complete the merger agreement that they signed. That is disappointing but now what occurred?

In this situation. JetBlue offered more money and presented a case that would add value to give them a competitive market. Frontier Airlines must evaluate the failure. They didn't convince Spirit Airlines of the value they bring at a price point. Maybe they weren't listening to the Spirit board when they wanted something different, like more airline control. Or it could have been that they couldn't demonstrate the ability a new company could do for its shareholders. Whatever it is, Frontier Airlines failed. Hopefully, they didn't blame management and fired everyone immediately. This would be an overreaction without exploring what occurred. Smart people research what happened and try to understand it.

In your failure that you wrote about above, was it with a relationship? Were you trying to be someone you aren't? With business: were you trying to do something that was outside of your capabilities? Or was it just not the right fit for your aspirations?

We need to explore and ask ourselves these questions. Answer them yourself.

Why did the failure occur?

Was it within my control?

Are there things that occurred were they related to weather, government, or politics?

Now that we have figured out what happened and why this occurred. If any is related to government, process or politics realize that things easily change in these organizations. That today your failure may have occurred because of people's person aspirations and when that person leaves office they change may occur again.

Step 2 – Approach:

When a failure occurs, there is an opportunity for a different approach. The approach is our way of looking at what occurred with some clarity to grasp better what happened. By understanding what occurred, we can look at how we approached (handled) the situation. Reviewing the situation from multiple angles could change our perspective on the situation.

Let's say two people broke up because the man was being jerky with his friends, and the woman wasn't feeling as valued. The man puts too much emphasis on his friends than on the relationship. He had a bad experience with a previous woman and was afraid to get hurt in the same way again. He had his past influence on his current relationship. They broke up, but he realized the errors in his ways. He decided that with his next relationship, he would try a new approach to open up his emotions. This new approach is an opportunity to try again to overcome his previous failure.

Great business people, entrepreneurs, and successful people don't take No for an answer. They focus on trying a new approach to open up that door by finding a new way of accomplishing the goal. It's challenging to get back up over and over, but those who do this can learn from their mistakes. I met a President of a small company who said he would never advertise for a position at his company. He would tell his employees & friends about any openings to see if someone would knock on his door. He would hire them if they did and showed him their worth. He found most of the employees were these go-to types who could handle multiple projects and change as needed.

Elon Musk has exploded rockers countless times on the launch pad at Space X test facilities. This didn't stop him; it empowered him to try harder. This drive is the critical approach you need at this stage. It's not always easy and worthwhile. But it's the area that sets people who will succeed apart from others.

We asked ourselves, How do you get this drive? What do you do?

- First, look at why you failed in the previous step—now understand this. How can you change your approach?

Changing your approach is looking at a situation, trying something similar then asking again. If I were going to ask for funding from a bank that turned me down the first time, I would drive to a different city or town to find the same or similar bank and then ask them for a loan.

Updating your presentation or selling your idea after a failure is the best way to get your idea across. Here is an example where a change worked:

A football player who has been going into investors wearing a suit and tie. Found that this formal attire doesn't work for him. He feels uncomfortable and not himself. Every presentation seemed off; he was touching his clothes and forgetting essential points.

We recommended that he find different professional clothes. The football player likes golf attire. In the following presentation, he wore lovely golf attire. Immediately when he got there, the loan manager started to ask him about golf. The football player is highly knowledgeable, and the manager and him bonded. When he finished mentioning the idea and getting a small investment. The loan manager was already printing out the paperwork so they could move to the loan process. This wouldn't have worked if my friend hadn't been himself.

You need to approach problems from failure as yourself. When you try to emulate someone else, people will know what is occurring, but it may fail.

What are the available approaches that you might change?

a) Communication - How did you communicate last? Did you email last? Maybe try phone or text? Change to a different method.

b) Project - Did your project miss deadlines, or did it seem that you/your team needed to be more organized? Ensure that your next project doesn't have any of this occur. Even go as far as doing the project a week early to show your passion for the project.

c) Technological - I was using software or technological product that was too advanced for me, and which might have caused the failure. Try a different software package or use something that can give you the answers without using technology.

Answer these questions to help you look within to determine what possible errors occurred and what you could do in the future.

What approach did you try when reaching out to people when the project failed?

What is your preferred communication method? Does it work in your position?

What new approach will you try to address this issue?

Now that you have figured out parts of the approach that didn't work. We are focusing on a new approach method that you identified. Applying this new method might or might not work, but by going through these questions a few times, you can figure out your best method of getting your ideas out there and utilize this for future discussions/presentations.

Here is the conversation I have in my head when this step doesn't work.

I ask myself, what did not work? For me, it's a lot about the conversation that arose. Was I able to demonstrate the value our company can bring to the situation? If not, then I couldn't show the value in a three-minute presentation. It might be me; if so, I bring someone else and have them share another aspect of the idea since what I shared didn't seem to resonate with the audience

Keeping a record of how you approach a problem is one of the best ways to know how to improve.

Step 3 - Improvements

We need to look at critical improvements to take away from this. This isn't about looking at the changes for a new approach; it improves our work to see what needs to be taken out when I deliver a pitch in the future or present an idea.

One thing that comes to mind in the improvements section is how people rely on PowerPoint, Canva, or Google Slides to give presentations. Most people tend to read off the slides, a terrible presentation habit that people need to adjust. But understanding this about yourself is essential. An improvement is that if you know the slides and use them as reference material, you focus more on the person or audience. The slides can be a considerable aid since they give background details and provide another way to sell your idea.

A second improvement is about change. When people give a second presentation, most people deliver the same presentation. That isn't going to provide you with the best results. It would be best to look at the presentation each time you give it and learn from your previous presentations. Changing one slide or removing redundant information makes the pitch better. I may want to ask myself, Is there a way of coming across differently with my speech pattern? Improvements done iteratively may be small, but many small changes result in more extensive results.

Explore this lets us ourselves a question about how we act.

What do people say about you that they like or don't like? (ie. too enthusiastic, voice too loud, talk too quickly, leg shakes, etc.) Write down your answer.

What did you write down? I would challenge you to improve this, make improvements from suggestions, and help people incorporate them into a larger strategy for change. This will help you turn what seemed like failure into success.

How can you make improvements? Is there something you can change? If so what is that thing that you would change?

This is the goal of the improvement section. By focusing on the minor improvements, we can change that would improve the overall. It could be as easy as getting up early, going to bed early, or exercising three times a week. Whatever they are, these minor improvements would help each of you overcome failure.

Step 4 - Lessons learned

What can I learn from this whole situation? Lessons are those hard truths you look at from the other sections to consider what you can know/teach yourself from the entire project.

One example that comes to mind is what is occurring with Twitter. Elon Musk purchased Twitter, then began to structure the organization to work differently. As part of the process, he laid off numerous employees within the company. Then he presented his ideas of how work should occur to other employees at Twitter, and many resigned from the company.

Suppose Elon is looking at this later on as a lesson-learned situation. I want to understand better what the employees want from the company. Then seek to appeal to their desires and goals. Learning their wants could help me craft a shared vision between his objectives and theirs. By focusing on this in the short term, you can make improvements without losing all the knowledge employees have gained through the years. Lessons Learned is a vital tool to use as a reflection place and helps us grow.

One lesson that I always consider is Thomas Edison. It took one thousand times to figure out how not to make a light bulb, and it worked on the one thousand and one. His lessons learned could be that it takes lots of persistence to do it correctly. The next time he wants to innovate this idea to something else, it should take less time since he learned the lessons from this journey.

What can I learn from this whole situation? Lessons are those hard truths you look at from the other sections to consider what you can know/teach yourself from the entire project.

How would you redesign a modern SUV (the most popular car type in the United States) because it's not energy efficient due to the height, it's less aerodynamic than a car, and it wastes gas/electricity due to wind drag?

Your answer doesn't matter, but you looking at it from an outsider's perspective. The perspective is essential when looking at our takeaways from a situation. This perspective technique helps us better understand the project we are working on. It is said that people only see the parts they are working on during a project, but when you ask a friend or colleague, they see something else. Lessons learned are best from another perspective since it opens up the idea to possibilities that I may have discarded due to constraints, which shouldn't bind us to lessons for the future.

More significant lessons that I learned from reviewing projects and failures.

1. Always approach a problem from someone else's perspective.

    Seeing it from the other person's perspective, it's not always about what's in it for them, which could be anything from money, control, or their doubts. We need to understand the other person's motivation.

    How do I do this? I need to research and design a person in my head. What are their motivations? Why are they in the positions they are in? How can they make a difference, and it's something they will invest in?

Researching companies' goals and products will show me their focus. Calling up people who work there may give me insights into their viewpoints and challenges. Collecting all this will help me to format a fictitious person I would use to see my failure differently.

2. Present so the audience comes up with your idea.

I struggle with this, but the ability to make suggestions or ask questions allows ideas to come up, bringing people along a specific path. The path or pitch you are going toward would be a direction where you lead them to find a solution which is your original idea. Instead of just telling them in the beginning, you have the audience figure it out themselves. How do you do this?

- You would present them with a list of questions that take them down a story or path that would help them get to similar conclusions that you are presenting.

- Focus on what they feel there is a need for this product or service.

- Demonstrate that you can offer them this in a way they might not have considered.

  For example: you could say "These two examples are ways I found that after reviewing presentations, that can improve our company outlook to stakeholders or investors. What other improvements could you add to the things you have learned?"

These four steps that are part of FAIL are a continuous process that keeps going in over and over, and it's not something that occurs only once. The best business entrepreneurs know they must continue going through this four-step process every time a setback occurs. It can be empowering to some and frustrating to others, but I have seen the value these bring to all situations.
Besides, this book has some interactive sections. I designed this exercise to help you understand and grasp the failure section.

Exercise 1:

You must pitch a new ride to Disney World. The new ride is called Water Immersion. You present the ride where riders will be completely submerged under the water for the whole ride. They must wear bathing suits and be seated in mechanical cars that give each person a specialized breathing machine. This machine will allow each person to breathe, experience, and enjoy the 15-minute loop while sitting in a railroad-type open-air car. As they go through this immersive experience, they will have Disney characters come up to them from underwater vehicles. They each tell a story about driving on the bottom of an African lake. The ride has no animals since it is based on Mickey, Minnie, Goofy, Donald, the seven dwarfs, and Cinderella.

- The pitch went great, at least. You thought it did.

- Disney returned and said no, this is too similar to other rides. Why would we want people underwater? That is just not us. The classic characters we are losing our copyright on Mickey soon; we need to think differently. They said, "This is the best you can come up with." They continued for 15 minutes; that was a long ride. How many people would you take at a time? It's different than we are charging extra for this attraction. Where would the people go for such a long period? Are they teleported somewhere to get to Africa, or is this simulated? We don't own that technology.

- What park would it be located in, Disney World filled with attractions? Are there alternative locations?

You must review the FAIL process steps and re-pitch, including your lessons learned.

David Ecker

Overcome Change

A critical aspect that entrepreneurs have developed that we all can take with us is their ability to overcome change. Change is a constant in your lives. Ever since technology came into existence at the turn of the 18th century, we have discovered that things are changing quicker than we can keep up with all the information. We all need to have some tips on how to overcome this change.

In this chapter, I focus on the methods that entrepreneurs utilize to overcome the constant change and pressure they are under when building organizations for success.

Change is similar to failure, but there are steps that people take to overcome it positively. It's also called failing forward. They can recover quickly, and we wonder how these people can continue to move forward after they fell flat on their faces. The only way I have found to do this is to start with the basics:

a) Good Team
b) Solid support system
c) Financial security
d) Expertise in the field

Having all these makes it easy to fail forward and keep moving. In this new post-pandemic way of work, things don't always work out the way we see them, but we need to deal with failures quickly and easily. When we do this, we can pivot to the next project quickly. The professionals that can rotate rapidly are the ones that will continue to overcome ideas in streamlined and focused methods.

How do you do this? We will discuss the four methods in this chapter and how they can be applied.

Good Team:

A good team is a group of individuals working together to support each other's efforts in the company. If you notice, I was specific that these people aren't working toward completing the project or objective. That is where most people in companies fail to see why teams work together. It's not about the company's goals but about the people within the organization who support each other no matter their level or position. It's a sense of community that is built within the company.

When a company focuses too much on the projects rather than the people, they lose community, which sometimes doesn't build a good team. This occurs because companies don't see the internal dynamic that occurs when a group of highly skilled professionals can achieve it by collaborating. True teams are about supporting each other no matter the goal.

Research has found that when you have a team focused on each other, no matter the project, this team can rapidly complete them. Management can throw any curve ball project at this team, and even if they don't know how to complete the task, they can learn, figure it out and accomplish it. This makes entrepreneurial teams different and more efficient than corporate teams.

Entrepreneurial teams have a passion, drive, and collaboration to achieve goals since they are focused on each other growth.

What are the qualities of this type of team?

Support System:

A sound support system is crucial for any entrepreneur. Difficult days occur, but when you can make a phone call to a family member or friend, they can get through those days more manageable. Polling entrepreneurs determine that when they have support within the company or outside, they can keep ideas progressing no matter the obstacle. This support makes it possible to change difficult days into opportunities.

The support system is also a cheerleader in their corner, no matter when good or bad results occur. This support system doesn't have to be family; it could be friends, relatives, colleagues, or acquaintances. No matter where the support system is, they are crucial in dealing with change.

Financial Security:

What is security? Most people want some financial security that, if they fail, they have something to return on. It's not consistent with entrepreneurs since some have come from nothing and achieved greatness. Others find that they are more comfortable leaping and selling their idea when they have financial funds available to catch them if they need it. An example is when a family member says you can always live in my basement if needed. It could be a bank that says you always have a line of credit or savings. No matter where this comes from or how it's developed. The security this gives allows entrepreneurs to take more risks in their businesses.

What security do you feel you need to go out on your own?

Expertise in the field:

What do you mean by expertise? The knowledge you have gained in a specific industry is critical to overcoming a change. This knowledge is the value you bring to work and gives you the confidence to be an expert in your area. For some people, if you are a teacher, you know how to educate kids, provide them with a sense of order and patience, and help them to grow by learning and applying this knowledge. This makes you, as a teacher, a valuable resource to schools since you can be effective where many other professionals won't.

Expertise is the application of knowledge that makes education the great equalizer in the world—learning to give you a perspective on understanding and completing tasks in various industries. An information technology professional may know how to solve issues when technology doesn't function correctly. This knowledge makes them valuable no matter the company they are employed in. This knowledge also allows them to use it to solve problems outside a company within their ventures.

Expertise is your fallback on how to overcome change because all of us, as individuals, bring something unique to our companies. This fallback is the safety that people need to overcome any change since, over any idea, things evolve. Still, industry knowledge allows you to weather changes as they occur and bring a sense of reasoning to the situation.

Summary:

These four areas are the core that entrepreneurs need to have in place when facing change in all aspects of the company, whether it's customer, product, or service. When we look at change through foggy glasses, it's easy to grasp that change is uncontrollable, but I'm afraid I have to disagree. Change can be empowering if you can help influence the change negatively or positively; you are at least able to feel some level of comfort. It may not be something that can be solved, but as people, change is always daunting at first, but once we dig into the difference, we can better understand and help overcome it.

David Ecker

Risk

Entrepreneurship is about taking a risk on an idea to see if there is an opportunity to develop it. What is a risk, and how do we handle it? When we think about the risk, we have to consider the chance we take on an idea. Some people see risk in how they feel about going to a casino, where you are betting money at a table or slot machine with a chance to win. I have played craps and poker; it's taking a risk with your money and an opportunity to win more money, but I don't see risk this way. I see this as gambling.

Risk is the chance you take and stand behind an idea you feel will bring opportunities. Risk is something that you see out to put your heart and soul into something that will benefit people. Gambling is the ability to take money to play a game that can give you a thrill which may or may not result in gaining additional money. You can control risk, whereas in gambling, control is with someone else, and you are just a participant. Risk is something you can manage and put effort into depending on your wants and desires.

Henry Ford had an idea to create a car that would move people with a gas-powered personal vehicle instead of the trains of the time. He took a risk with his idea to build a car with an engine. A century later, after his initial idea, millions relied on his car as a primary mode of transportation on the planet. The engine-powered notion is used in personal vehicles, buses, motorcycles, the military, and trucks to move people/goods. All from his initial idea and design. We may not all drive a Ford-branded car, but his brand still exists today. This is an example of how an entrepreneur takes a risk on their idea. They may put it all on the line for a chance of success.

Where does risk come from?   The dictionary defines risk as exposure to hazard or danger.   Do we knowingly expose ourselves to danger? Would we walk into a burning building with the off chance we will come out the other side alive?   Most of us wouldn't take the chance, but that is where these individuals stand apart. They see the burning building not as a chance to lose their life. They see it as an opportunity that will give them a chance to show off their skills in a new way.   These individuals are called Entrepreneurs for that specific reason. They are willing to put themselves out to support their idea.

We need to understand how risk-averse you are as we explore the opportunities available to us as individuals. In the questions below, let's explore your choices to glimpse your mindset.

Let's see how you handle risk. Answer these questions on the scale in the corresponding chart below. Complete your answers in the table below after reading each question before answering the following question.

1. If you were standing next to someone, a tree branch was falling. Do you grab them from a stranger and move them out of the way, or do you move only?

2. Your boss asked you to move some boxes that he needs to be moved today. But it's raining, windy and cold. Do you still move the boxes from one building to another today, which is a 10-minute walk between them, or do you do it in the morning? Your supervisor went home and isn't supposed to be in tomorrow.

3. Your friend wants to tour his new office, but it's still under construction; the supervisor said only construction personnel, and there are posted signs that stay kept out. How likely are you to go to the work site?

4. Your mom wants a lily plant for her birthday. You go to the greenhouse where she told you to purchase the lily, and the greenhouse is open, but no one is there. You say hello loudly, but no one answers. You decide to walk around the store and find the perfect lily. Your Mom's birthday is tomorrow, and the greenhouse is only open for another 10 minutes and will be closed tomorrow. No one is in the whole store for you to purchase the lily. Do you wait until tomorrow when someone is there so you can properly pay for it and tell Mom you couldn't buy it? Or do you take the lily without anyone knowing?

5. You are in a band performance on Sunday; today is Friday. You find out at 7 pm that you are the only available drum player, and you must be able to perform all the pieces for the performance on Sunday morning. You are going to be out of town on Saturday. On a scale of 1 to 5. Would you show up on Sunday without practicing?

	Strong Disagree	Disagree	Neither Agree or Disagree	Agree	Strongly Agree
Scale	1	2	3	4	5
1. Move the person from the falling branch					
2. Don't move the boxes today					
3. Give your friend a tour of your new office					
4. Take the plant from the store					
5. Don't Practice Drums					

Based on these answers, you should have a total score.
- Below 10 demonstrate you are risk-averse.
- Between 10-20, you are like most people; sometimes, you take a risk and play it safe.
- Between 20-25, you are a risk taker and fall into the category that you might be entrepreneurial

Now that we have determined where you stand. Let's say you are in the 20+ category. You have an opportunity to be an entrepreneur.

What are the steps you would take to continue to develop your risk?

Entrepreneurs ask themselves if they can use their money and time for this idea. Most people who start a business usually start by investing their own money. If you don't have money, that's ok. You would have to go to your family to see if they will give you the startup funds necessary to take a risk on your idea. When they approach this idea with a positive attitude, we know that they are willing to put all their heart and soul into it.

As we look at risk and your risk tolerance, we need to think more about the steps in taking a risk.

There is a simple formula that exists when people who are wanting to take a risk.

Are you willing to take a chance on an idea? If your answer is yes. We need to focus on the three aspects of taking a risk:

a) Time

b) Guidance

c) Funding

Time:

This is the ability to find time to devote to this idea. It's either waking up early, quitting your current job, staying late or some other time. This time needs to be your first consideration on any new venture. The time available will put some boundaries on how you begin and help you focus on the core aspects of your idea.

I heard about a father who wanted to start a company offering training programs on financial software, but he only knew the one that his current company utilized. He knew that he would have to learn a few others. So how did he do this?

He had two kids at home and a wife who depended on him daily to bring in an income. He could have just given up the idea, but that wasn't the type of person he was. He set his alarm for 1 hour before everyone got up in the morning. He read books and learned the software. He also found time each weekend when is wife would watch the kids for two hours so he could develop his idea.

This support gave him the opportunity and time to work on his idea. Are you an early riser? Are you someone who stays up late? Are you able to multitask at work? Do you have breaks or time off from your primary source of income? Are you planning to quit your position?

W hen time do you have to devote to your idea?

Guidance

Guidance has one person around us to encourage and motivate us to continue with our idea. Ideas are difficult to turn into a reality, and the only way this occurs is with a group that will help you achieve. Guidance comes from one person. This is different from the support system from the previous chapter, the advice of one person who is there for you as a partner or best friend. They are there to help you get your idea going, tell you the truth about when things go well, and also be there to celebrate when things fail. Without that person, things sometimes go in many directions, which can cause opportunities to be missed.

If you think about Albert Einstein, who said," I have not failed a thousand times, and I successfully found one thousand ways not to make a light bulb."

I found this person is the one I can call at 5 am with an idea; they would always listen. This friend/partner is your help with taking the opportunity. Risk is about calculations, and having someone understand the math necessary to take a risk is vital. We sometimes want to take a chance because emotion tells us it's the right idea. We need to put emotion aside to look at the finances and if the idea is attainable.   This person is the one that will be there in your life and help you navigate your journey in entrepreneurship.

Funding

Funding is always considered the most important by people because they look at this as the only way to get an idea moving is to have the money to start the idea. Funding was the last aspect I needed in all companies I have created, and I was more focused on the concept and development than funding. When I needed money, I found it, and so can you. It's important, but when you start small and look at things as small steps, it only takes a little funding to move your idea to the next level.

It's easy to think you can start without money, but that is different. Money is an essential driver in all businesses, but so many people on the internet developed apps, social media, restaurants, and products started with no money. They just went out and figured it out.

How do you go out and figure it out? My best piece of advice is to Ask. You will be so surprised when you ask people for help. I would only ask people for money if you ask them to bounce ideas, offer you their time, help you to build something, or even give you a shout-out on social media. People love to do this. It's this aspect where funding will eventually come from, but you need to ask to be able to succeed in this step.

Summary:

Based on these three principles of Time, Guidance and Funding anything is possible for an Entrepreneur. As we continue to strive forward on our journey, we need to know that risk may be the cornerstone of any good idea.

Exercise 2:

We all need to learn how to ask for something that will cost us nothing. This is a strange concept since we always feel we should pay for a product or service. It is possible to get something without the exchange of money.

In this exercise you are going to ask at least 15 small or medium based companies for them to give you advice, product or service at no charge. A small or medium based company are more local or organizations that aren't franchise or big box stores. (such as Target or Walmart) Your goal is to ask for something that can be freely given by explaining to them you are learning about entrepreneurship. This will involve some persuasion and taking a risk.

For each interaction that you have with a company, you need to collect the follow information.

- Name of the Company, What the company does, what you asked for and why, and the result.

Did you get anything for no cost?

If you didn't why or why not?

Generating Ideas

How do you go about generating an idea for a business? Most people think new ideas appear in their minds while you sleep, which is not the case. Ideas come from every day when we are working or seeing broken processes at companies, and we know how to fix the problem.

This section focuses on entrepreneurs who want to start something but don't know where to begin. They feel they have the skills necessary to have a company but lack a concrete idea of what to do. You can do this by looking at yourself or your team to determine what areas you might be able to help the industry.

Here are the starting areas where you can look at industries you are aware of: Using these prompts to look at them from a critical standpoint.

a) Look at the markets or industries you know. What are they doing to complete their work? Is this a repeatable process or something that can be improved?

b) Research the industry to understand what has changed in the last 20 years. Do you see something that is missing that you can add to make it better for the consumer? This is looking at historical change and where they are now— thinking from a customer who utilizes the services of the industry.

c) Industries have lots to offer the customers but sometimes focus on what is profitable instead of what is needed. Is there something people need but isn't being offered?

a. Cleaning supplies, for example, have many different manufacturers, but they may need something that would be ideal for high-traffic flooring. You might have a friend that knows of this. He suggests this is an area customer have requested, but there hasn't been a solution.

b. This gap in the marketplace may give you an edge over the competition. This gap you may have discovered for high-traffic areas could be a potential windfall if you develop your prototype correctly.

Example:

Panera bread way of improving the atmosphere for customers. Panera bread an upscale healthy fast-food chain restaurant. An excellent offering of products in a relaxing atmosphere. Remote work arrangements have had some people look for places like Panera to work. Panera is missing a quiet area for phone calls or meetings. This could be a gap in the marketplace for a telephone booth-type area that is quiet and semi-private, where you can add to these restaurants to take a meeting without distributing other patrons.

What is the one thing you see in a market that you know well that is missing or wish was different? *A market is defined as an industry from gas/oil, health foods, transportation, technology, finance, etc.

We will cover three aspects of generating ideas. Trends, Passion and Gaps are part of a larger perspective of idea generation.

Trends:

Trends occur, and they can help us predict where the next step of an industry is proceeding. If we know some advanced knowledge, we can use this to build a company. What is a trend? A trend is an industry or organizational change occurring over time that will influence how the industry processes or provides a solution. The elimination of Cable TV is a trend that is changing slowly, and young people are no longer interested in traditional television. We all see trends but can we see them early enough to act on them? That is the unknown question.

- There has been a trend of replacing desktop computers with laptops and now laptops with mobile phones. If you see this trend, can you offer something that will help people be more productive? This is an apparent trend, but it continues to occur and has lots of social impact in the first world.

- A follow-up to this trend. You ask a customer what they think about desktops going away. One customer said, "I would love to eliminate my computer and have a device that I plug my phone into a computer monitor with a keyboard and mouse. Then I could have everything whenever I wanted." Wow, there is an idea. Is this a trend or concept you can get behind?

W hat trend do you see happening over the next 3-5 years in a specific industry?

Passion:

Do you have the desire to make a change that is needed? Higher education should be required to change its teaching practices from a traditional theory to a lecture model. It is not ideal for students to sit, take notes and repeat the knowledge memorized back on an exam. This misses the practical knowledge; this is why more universities are integrating active learning into classrooms. It adds a different level of expertise to education. Some schools, such as Western Polytechnical Institute, have switched teaching to a hands-on approach.

This is an industry trend in that educators may see opportunities and desire to improve student's learning outcomes. Required is passion from professors, administrators, and staff to make the change may be difficult, and some will be comfortable since what always worked shouldn't be changed. This is why specific industries are stagnant.

Passion change is something that takes time to happen. But passion increases the ability of a chance to happen. When management or an industry sees individuals excited about a change, it becomes more relevant and usually is talked about among its consumers. We all need to understand that Passion is one aspect that generates ideas for solutions.

What are you passionate about in your life? List at least two things. Could you change something in this industry or area?

Market Gaps:

Gaps in the marketplace exist because there isn't enough revenue for the larger companies to compete in that space, or people haven't found a necessary solution. All marketplaces have these gaps; if you can fill that gap, you will have a business on your hands.

Example:
Many years ago, we saw a gap in the marketplace that people in the United States West Coast desired fresh Maine Lobster. We worked with local fishermen to design a way of shipping this to them. This was when the Internet was young, but there was a need customer wanted Maine lobster and were unable to receive it. We researched and determined there were enough customers to support a business.

Anytime these gaps exist, entrepreneurs with passion will find some way to close the gap either with their company, competitor, or a very different solution. No matter how you go, you are helping the customer, which is the job of someone who helps others.

Whaat Gaps do you see in the marketplace or area you are
engaged with? These could be small. To figure out a gap,
complete this exercise. You are writing down your answer to one
of these in the space provided.

Some people need a starting point to find gaps that need a solution.
Here are four prompts that may help you with the previous
question.

    a)   From the list of interests above, write down one broken
          thing.

    b)   From living in your home, what is one thing you wish was
          an easier way of completing that task?

    c)   Do you have a way of improving your laptop?

    d)   Is there a need in Kenya for something that we have
          already implemented?

These are a few ways that people generate ideas. Ideas come from
research, time, and trial and error. They don't start as big ideas;
usually, it's small concepts that, as they develop, things evolve into
something bigger. These generating ideas help start a business
since they can take a picture and turn it into a business.

Generating ideas helps any entrepreneur know what interests them,
use their existing knowledge, and learn how they can improve
upon it for something else for themselves.

Foundation

Any Entrepreneur or business leader must think about the how their journey's will start that they can build upon. We are focused on how Ford, Amazon, Microsoft, and Exxon-Mobile have gotten to where they are to achieve their great goals of delivering their products/services to the world, but we need to remember that they all started from somewhere. The foundation necessary for any starting leader needs to think about the ideas and process to move forward.

An Entrepreneur is a fancy word that exists in our ecosystem. It is our way of saying the person who founded a company. They took an idea and developed this idea. But what did they do? How did they start? What core foundation elements exist for each person when they start?

This chapter or area covers the foundation necessary for any business to begin. The focus here is on mission and vision, and we need to develop these in a specific way that would help us keep our focus and strategy to make the company a success. How do you start?

Mission:

The mission/purpose should be easy since it defines what you intend to do and how you plan to accomplish it.

Here is a one-page document I wrote in 2014 for the Innovation Lab concept at Stony Brook (it was a concept to form what is now known as makerspaces but didn't exist at that time)

Example:

Summary of Goals and Objectives:

To provide a prototype, development, innovation, and collaboration space for Stony Brook University students and researchers. This would allow them to work hand and hand to innovate and develop new ideas that can be experimented with within a campus location. Our goal would bring partnerships with the College of Business students to help with marketing, business planning, and company development to allow small businesses to be started right here on Long Island. This effort will support the local economy and the governor's Startup New York ideas.

What are we doing?

We are working to build partnerships and collaborations with various departments/institutes throughout the campus. In doing this, we understand their need to provide a more well-rounded location that can include their vision. In doing this, we would develop a community of Innovation at Stony Brook University.

Community:

The goal of the Innovation Lab is to have a place where this community of students, researchers, and staff can take ideas from concept to a physical prototype. To provide a complete and welcoming community, we would put together general rules that would guide the lab area. This can ensure proper communication among all of the community, as well as open up ideas for startup businesses.

Values for the Innovation Lab
- Communicate
- Collaborate
- Innovate

This example is what I would like you to develop for any new company. It's a 1-page document that describes the product/service. Our idea is to create a space where a cross-cutting part of the community can utilize the space. In that opening line we also told you the plan and whom we are focusing on for customers. If you can do this upfront, it helps people understand your idea quickly.

The example document took a few weeks to develop since multiple people reviewed, revised and gained feedback. Having this document as our purpose allowed us to have a starting point for launching the idea. Especially when you are beginning a venture, there is a lot to do. We usually have timelines, paperwork, financials, product/service creation, and technology issues to get the company created; startups can stay focused with this document.

The community/customers were a critical aspect that must be part of our conversations. We had them in our purpose document to showcase how much value we brought to them. As we began to bring on employees, we found that sharing this document gave them the knowledge and our founding principles.

A mission is what you are doing for the customers.   The task can be vague since it will allow you to have ideas that can be branched out within the company.

Amazon's mission statement - "We strive to offer our customers the lowest possible prices, the best available selection, and the utmost convenience" From the 2019 SEC filing.

Amazon sometimes uses its shorter statement, "Amazon is focused on Lowest Prices."
- Let's look at the "Lowest prices" part of the statement. They say this is a focus when you look at their website, app, or other, and the price is highlighted and more prominent for easy viewing.
- They highlight tons of products that cover a wide selection of offerings.
- The "utmost convenience" is the delivery. We all know they have a fleet of trucks that do deliveries and can usually deliver to your door.

We can see how the parts of the mission are showcased at their company through a website or store. It only covers some things. Amazon makes 14% of its revenue from amazon web services, but this isn't listed in its mission. That's ok; not everything needs to be included.

Why do you think it's absent?

Amazon doesn't list it since it's unnecessary because they offer the lowest prices on whatever they offer. In addition, the amazon web service is more business and business-focused, which is only sometimes in need of a mission statement. They focus their mission statement on their customer-facing business. It may need to be more specific, but it's a standard mission statement that allows them to go in different directions as they develop. Most people need to update their mission statements.

COCA-COLA mission statement - "To refresh the world in mind, body, and spirit, to inspire moments of optimism and happiness through our brands and actions, and to create value and make a difference."

That is a long, run-on sentence.

Are they trying to do something different with this statement?

With this mission statement, they are focused on the customer experience that brings them joy when using their products. It's focused on something other than them as a specific product they offer but specifically on the emotion that is felt. Does that make their products different? It allows them to bring any drink that provides that feeling into their company, which has allowed them to focus on various waters, sodas, and related products. It's brilliant if you think about it.

They didn't focus on a specific product or price, and they were thinking about how people have an emotional connection. They have included this into their marketing/branding with polar bears to make you have a relationship with them.

These two mission statements are very different, but mission statements are just things that are made up, correct? They are made up, but most are the basis for any company to achieve greatness. It could be as easy as bringing computers to every household or more complex. But we need to define this as a thought process in our development.

We need to think about the company's mission and how it got where they are now. As I think about this, I define the mission in simplistic terms. It's what you want to achieve in your industry, and it should be easy to remember and be focused on what you do for your clients or customers. To do this, think about your simple objective.

An example of an easy-to-remember mission statement from a tea company is "Making the world smile each day with a cup of tea." It's toward the point, but some marketing is thrown into it. At the same time, their simplistic mission is bringing their tea to the world. We would have to assume this company is a grower of teas, package them, and deliver them. Everyone in the company knows what they will do and how their jobs will be related. This is where small business has an advantage over large companies. They can have all employees know the mission and be guided toward the objective. Large companies have people focused on a position unrelated to the mission.

Mission statements, like others, sometimes don't tell what they do, and it needs to be precise. But we need to think simply like the tea company. This is where we look at the foundation skills we need to consider for your new company.

The foundation is the building block that makes us create a startup. To start a company, we need to have one that gives our employees and our clear understanding. I always find a mission to be the statement I go back to whenever I need clarification on our objectives.

Now - Take a minute and think about it. Throw out all the fancy adjectives and statements. In the most core simple terms:

What do you do? What would you like a new company to do for its clients?

What is your objective?

This can be hard for people. You Did it! You got it down to your simple terms.

Explain your business to your 80-year-old grandmother in 4 sentences or less with emotion.

Now that we summed up our objectives and explained this to your grandmother. We can begin to write your mission statement. You have an aim which is the core part of your mission, that doesn't change over time. Do we want to add any emotional connection that we may have included in the statement to our grandmother? By combining these, we can write our mission statement to deliver what is expected from the new startup company.

Write your Mission statement:

Vision Statement:

The vision statement is what you plan to achieve in the future. To do this, you must have some aspects of your purpose or mission document to guide you. Vision is what you can do if you can influence everyone.

In our Innovation Lab example above, I included three values Communicate, Collaborate and Innovate. We wanted to focus on these values for the organization.

a) Communicate – Clear written and verbal communication with our customers and our employees

b) Collaborate – Working together across colleges, areas, and groups to build this organization. We focused on bringing the College of Engineering, College of Business, Division of Information Technology, and the Provost office together. As well as student groups from clubs, different disciplines, and various experiences. By including this, we had a welcoming open thought process for our future.

c) Innovate. - Always evolving to change something every few months or every year. We felt that if this organization stayed stagnant, it wouldn't be able to keep up with technology and ever-evolving changes in the business and engineering fields.

Focusing on these values gave us a foundation that allowed us to ask ourselves when new ideas came up, and we could look at our values as guidance. The values helped us set the foundation for our vision.

Goals:

We now need to consider the goals you would like to accomplish over the next 3-5 years. Professor talks about goals as the objective we would like to achieve, like graduating from college, getting a well-paid job, or creating a company that makes hot liquid stay hot for 10 hours. Anything is attainable, and a goal is a statement that defines your focus. We need to put down some plans for your new startup. Suppose you don't have any guesses. Guessing at least it gives you guidance on how to accomplish this. Do you have a goal of selling 1000 units? Having 100 customers? Making a $10,000 profit?

Write your goals for 3-5 years from now.

We now have goals and values that will be the basis for our next topic.

We need to consider how to write your Vision statement. A vision statement is a future state and the goals of the company. It's where you would like to be and accomplish. It focuses not solely on what you are doing, as the mission statement is but is usually more aspirational.

Based on your goals, values, and strategies you want to achieve in a few years. We use mission statements as our current state and vision statements as our future. By thinking of them in the present/future, we can distinguish the difference between them.

Here are some example vision statements:

- <u>Nike</u> - *Bring inspiration and innovation to every athlete.*

- <u>McDonald's</u> - *Being the best quick service restaurant. Providing outstanding service, quality, and value.*

- <u>Ted Talks</u> - *Spread ideas*

- <u>Uber</u> - *We ignite opportunity by setting the world in motion.*

These examples are short-to-point statements; they all look at a significant idea and purpose from the mission statement. As you review these, think about what you want to achieve, this is key for your vision.

W rite your vision statement.

This chapter focused on the foundational documents and statements needed for any company business plan, website, or selling point. We have these statements as our foundation (cement for a house); we can only build the rest with these documents. You will use this to build upon this book's other aspects. Think about how these were developed by knowing your objectives, goals, and values. These are key for you as you build your startup

Customer Perspective

Entrepreneurs need to focus on the customer viewpoint as they work to design and implement their products/services. There are times when you do a new service where you are offering tutoring services via video conferencing. Still, the customer is interested in something other than this since they spend much time on the computer daily. By looking at it from a customer's perspective, you can get more information to ensure that you focus on the customer.

Too many entrepreneurs make products for their use and personal use, but it is different from a product used by everyone. Focusing on the customer from the start, you are starting to understand their need and desire for your product. You must work with the client/customer to see their use of the idea to succeed. Failure is good, but we need to look at it from a customer's standpoint, only sometimes from your point of view. The initial ideas are good to have to solve a problem that we are happening, but when we try to branch the business out, we will need to adjust since everyone may have different issues.

An example that comes to mind is my Apple iPad. The iPad tablet computer is an additional device for most technology users. Most of us have mobile phones and a laptop/computers. Why would they need an iPad? Apple thought this would be a device that they could use for work or careers. Unfortunately, in the form it was released, it was a device that gave a larger screen but needed more functionality. It replicates the Apple iPhone if you have one of those devices. So why did they release it? They released it to meet a specific niche of customers who wanted a larger screen that was portable to do leisure activities. I love my iPad, but as the iPhone gets bigger, I have less use for the iPad.

How would you enhance this product if you were Apple?

I would talk to my customers to understand what they need. They may need a lightweight device with a large screen. I could use a larger screen device with a keyboard or an excellent speech-to-text solution to review lectures, work on presentations and interact with email for extended periods than my iPhone's quick replies.

The Apple iPad meets some of my needs since it has a larger screen, but I have purchased a lightweight external keyboard that can be used via Bluetooth for all my work. It would be better if this was all integrated into someone's fashion, and some models of the iPad are not experimenting with a combo package. But it's extra money, and the keyboard is cramped. I wanted a larger keyboard to quickly type multiple book pages into my notes and not have any fatigue caused by smaller keyboards. The portability was excellent, but I returned to my laptop for longer work.

If Apple had done more research, they would have found numerous customers like me that need this functionality without wanting to carry our heavy laptops with us for every journey. The Apple iPad has a niche for portability, but its capabilities are limited, and I advise them to make more customer discovery before releasing a new version.

From this example, the customer perspective is key to getting the product right and how it can solve a problem. How do you get customer perspective? A few proper methods have been working for years, and I will outline them below to show you how companies conquer this.

a) Focus groups — Ask a group of people within your audience and ask them to give you feedback. Usually, you give them some incentive, such as a small dollar figure or a gift for participating, and I have seen it where they offer coffee and tea too. The motivation isn't something that has to be grand, just simple.

- The focus group method is a vital aspect. You must know your audience correctly before you bring in this group.

- The audience is your core group that will utilize the service/product. What is this? Here is an example of a specific audience: It's a group of 18-25 years old with an income of less than 40K and who are in college. Some people will break down audiences that include race, gender, and even if they are specific technology (Android mobile phone users)

- This information allows you to be specific for your customer's perspective and get invaluable details not achieved in other ways.

b) Surveys - This is a method used by numerous companies, and they design a pre-written survey, either emailing it or asking at the end of the event to gain feedback. This method gives lots of results, like Amazon reviews, but most people find that the input begins with negative and then switches to positive.

- There are better solutions for gaining feedback than this. It can run into issues because you are asking specific questions and may need additional details from the customer.

- Since the owner/product specialist designs questions, they are focused on hearing specific parts that might be missing in the opportunities for change/improvement that could help.

- These are standard, and a response rate of 20% is impressive. You have to consider this, so you may need to distribute thousands to get accurate results.

c) Interviews - This method is where you ask people about their thoughts on the product or service. This seems strange in social media and all things happening over the Internet. It's very effective if you ask the right questions. People love to give feedback, even negatively, for you to capture valuable data.

  - This method is efficient when you can get in front of a group of your audience. Presenting the idea quickly (3 minutes or less), letting them try it, and giving feedback are worthwhile.

  - The reason why I like this method is first to look at their facial reactions. Are they happy? Sad? Confused? Interested? Bored. This will tell you something before you even start listening to the person.

Next, are the answers to the question. "What did you like most about the product/service?" If they said nothing, you could ask for a follow-up; this will give you details you can't get from other methods. In addition, if they have blank stares, that tells you something too. You need to get your message across to the group.

a) Surprising the people. This surprising method gives you their first impressions; this is sometimes the opening that we need to understand if they will make the purchase or not. The technique shows customers something they didn't expect by lifting a box or removing a curtain. This method helps you know how they relate to the product/service. It demonstrates the initial impression and presents opportunities to change the product for enhancements. The outcome was a bouncing ball that always bounces back from the ground with the same force. By giving them this ball, you discover it always has more power on the return because everyone seems to throw it on the ground. They are surprised and taken back by the speed as it comes back to them. This demonstrates that we may want to dampen the ball so it comes back at a different force placed on it. This will exceed consumers' expectations and purchase additional balls for kids.

This method gives you flexibility with the questions since you can go in multiple directions that depend on how the interview progresses. You will find some people that would like to share lots of ideas while others are just there for the freebie. Anyway gives you valuable knowledge on the next steps in marketing your product or service.

Exercise 3:

Design a 2-minute pitch that sells a new snow plow to the people in Maine who live with two feet of snow on the ground each year. They get snow at least every two weeks from December - March. What would your 2-minute pitch be to convince them to purchase your new snow plow? Hint: Think about the customer.

Competitor research

This last method is invaluable. What competitors exist in this industry sector? If there are, what are they doing with the customers? Knowing what they are doing helps you understand the uniqueness of your product. Learning about competitors can give you a specific place in the industry and help you know where your product should be positioned for maximum exposure.

a) Research what they are doing with their product or service. Are they able to help people, and do they make a profit? If they are profitable, there is an opportunity to copy what they are doing in a different way to bring your idea to a customer. Copying isn't making an exact duplicate but emulating their processes with your product, so you are meeting the customer's expectations.

b) Ask your direct competitors: Some competitors are open about sharing their methods and ideas. They do this because it lets them know about upcoming products. Be upfront when you reach out to them if you have a similar product. I have heard of competitors that lie; then, when the competitor finds out, they are upset and can make it more difficult in specific sectors since they flood the market with their products at a lower price than yours.

c) Find a competitor in a different market. I have a competitor that works out of Australia. We talk regularly about methods and questions to compare notes. Our collaboration works well since we are in different markets but can help each other achieve similar goals.

d) Library - Go to the library, and use their databases to research the industry. You are seeking any information that can help develop a complete customer perspective. Libraries are invaluable sets of knowledge on current events, past events and how their intersection will help us move our new products to market. Libraries also have databases on customers from demographics based on location, and this can help form your image of a perfect customer.

e) Find a Chief Executive Officer (CEO): Ask a CEO of a larger company that works in your business's sector and ask them for advice or information that may help you get started. You will be surprised at how many will respond with some details. CEOs have a different perspective since they think on a strategic level rather than on an individual product/service level. These CEOs like to mentor people; by reaching out, you can be one of the people they mentor.

How would you find the customer's perspective on a new drink called "Refresh Me"? It's a Sugar-Free flavoured water drink to give people the perspective that they are having an alcoholic cocktail without having one during the day. They would like to introduce Tequila Sunrise, Mojito, and Margarita flavours. List the steps you would take and write up a customer perspective for this drink. Please include as many details as possible so you can describe the person to a colleague so they can vividly picture this person walking along the street.

As you can see, the customer perspective is involved but allows an entrepreneur to understand the customers needs better. If you are going to achieve results, ensuring that the customer wants the product is just as important as the product you are designing. Too many young entrepreneurs think it's all about the product but understanding the customer ensures you are selling something they will utilize.

Marketing

People gravitate to social media whenever you say Marketing, but it's more than that. It's how people sell or share their product or service with potential customers. Social media is more than just that; it is the connection we are looking for to interface with our family, friends, and acquaintances when they aren't physically in the same place. We have all developed over the last 20 years into global citizens. Where we have friends worldwide, our reach for marketing can also be global, but understanding whom you want to reach is vital before you embark on any marketing plan.

The primary definition of marketing is the ability to get your product or service to the eyes of your customers. Marketing is more expansive than a specific platform or service. We need to do research and gain knowledge to implement an effective strategy. We will demonstrate some research through the chapters on customer perspective and networking.

Marketing is to ensure your customer knows that your product/service exists to be used to solve a problem. With so many ideas that exist, by setting the appropriate marketing strategy, you can inform others about your solutions. Marketing has countless classes on the techniques, plans, and development of those who need intense work in the field. We can hardly do any justice to marketing in this chapter. Still, we will approach it from an entrepreneur's perspective to ensure the basics are available to anyone interested in taking their product to market.

Marketing for Entrepreneurs is the ability to get your product/service out to the consumers in a new way that will highlight your unique perspective on the product/service. If you look at how others use marketing, we will see billboards, mail newsletters, television, social media, email, and phone calls. All these methods work, or they would still need to do them. But we must understand how to get our product to our customers. Just picking one of these randomly is like throwing money to the wind and expecting it to fly back to you.

You worked on identifying your audience in the customer perspective chapter; now, we need to reach them.

What are three things that stand out about your product or service?

Now that you have the three things that make you different, we need to figure out the best way of getting your message out to your audience. I will go over the various marketing places where you can deliver your message with some insights, but before we do that, you need a one-line description of what you are selling. Examples could be: A service that offers high schools the ability to pitch in Division 1 schools, a STEM toolbox of models you put together, A subscription service to indie music arts and interviews, etc

What is the one line that describes your business?

$1200 and a Dream

Marketing Avenues:

1. In Person

How to reach them through your connections? Are there any unique aspects of your audience that you can contact directly? People who sell software to university students will reach out to faculty and ask them to give a lecture or talk in their class. These people allow them to give information on the topic being taught and highlight their product/service to their target audience.

  a) Another method is giving away something free to the audience. Hotels may be interested in a unique soap enhancing the client's skin, and Lower-end hotels would not be interested since they are focused on a bargain for the room they give their clients.

  b) Upscale hotels might love a free complimentary custom-made soap because it can offer a unique feel and smell that would set them apart from their competitors. It would be best if you got in the door, but that is your market. Get those customers to use the product and then purchase directly from you.

  c) To reach this audience, you have to focus on them. Look for ways to interact with them in person. Networking helps with this since they can introduce you to others that can connect you to new friends.

2. Social. Media.

This is the go-to for many firms that want to market their products to a wider audience.

  a) It's an excellent avenue for getting your product to many people. But you have to target small subsets to get the most exposure. I find that when using social media, focus on your sub-set from your customer. This will help you achieve the best results.

b) If you have a cute ad or video that can make people re-share your idea, then you can use this to increase exposure, but increasing exposure doesn't always drive sales. It's just getting your idea or name out to a larger group. Sometimes you need to ensure you have the right customers even if you have a million views.

c) Social media is effective, but you have to build a following that is at least two thousand people before you get to a broader audience that is interested in following the messages you are working to deliver.

d) Research which social media platform to utilize for your audience. I am an Instagram and might target Males 24-34-year-olds with an income of $150,000 or more. That are professionals looking to develop their careers. Instagram may or may. Not be an ideal place for this audience. Research is important to ensure your marketing to the right person.

e) Engagement is the other key with social media; not only you may have followers. Getting comments from the community is a feedback method that brands like since they know you have a real community. A tip here is to make sure you engage on others' post in the niche you are working within. If you post on videos and posts people see your name. If they find your comment interesting, they may look up your profile.

f) The downside of social media from a business perspective it takes time away from other parts of building your business. Time is a valuable thing that we need to consider when we begin marketing on any media.

I look at social media as a long-term strategy since you need to gain followers and the more you are a respected authority, the more engagement you will see in your process or services.

3. Radio or Television Advertising.

This is the older, time-true method of reaching people who listen to the radio in their cars or watch television shows. It may or may not have its place, depending on your product.

a) This type of marketing depends on your audience. If your audience is older adults that interact that are homebound, this is the right market.

b) This can be effective but costly. In general, the ads have to be cute and get your point across quickly to work.

c) I have seen people advertise in smaller markets such as Syracuse, NY or Bowling Green, Kentucky, since their product has a reach to that audience. This advertisement may cost less, and the ad will be more effective. This is because fewer people will see the marketing, and when you are in a large market like NYC, your advertisement will be lost among the other competitors in the city market.

d) One thing that still works in smaller markets is personal advertising. Joe Still car dealership with a big discount on a car then a brick fell on the car. Is cute and surprising but people find it works. Smaller markets have very different aspects then larger docile media that is global.

e) Another trick here is that evening and overnight may work for you. Some of the overnight ads may be seen by a small audience, but the ones that are up are usually focused.

Overall this can be complex and difficult to manage without an agency but the cost is usually a defining factor. That moss young entrepreneurs forget about due to the cost. But I have seen it be very effective when you have a unique message and targeting.

4. Radio Advertising only

Small-market radio stations work well if you can research the audience. Usually, you can have an announcer help read your advertisement. An announcer read is cheaper than creating an ad. It will grow your audience and sometimes drive sales if your audience is listening.

- Radio speaks to people in cars. Your ad should keep that in mind.

5. Call to Action

A call to action is what most marketing people now find as the focus for all good advertising. It's the opportunity of having the customer do something to connect with you or your products. It's either with a website, social media handle or QR code to have the customer reach do something with their smartphone. This is something most marketing people utilize. What is that call action you want people to do? Entrepreneurs have an idea that can get people to do something. Common Call to Action that small companies implement:

a) Sign up for the newsletter

b) Purchase a mug for .99 cents

c) Send an email to get a free guide

d) Offer a gift card if you act now within the first 10 seconds to do some action.

e) Informational commercials sell you a pot for $29.96, but you don't only get the pot; you get a salad dish, plates, and a free fry pan. The free stuff enticed you to purchase. This works!

Your objective of grabbing the customer and then real them in is the objective. The call to action is a big practice with the interactive internet. The more interaction, the more reach you have with your products.

6. Traditional newspaper advertising

This has less appeal nowadays because it reaches less of an audience. Most people get their news from the internet, smartphones or social media. Companies that still utilize this say its good for getting your message or your name out there for exposure only; it may not bring in sales.

7. News exposure (on any platform).

This is the ideal objective since if you get interviewed by someone is a great way to gain exposure. Most news agencies share their stories and are picked up but other media broadcasts. Companies love this ideal exposure since it's very inexpensive and has the potential to reach new and existing customers. How do you do this?

a) Find your way of getting an article written about you.

b) If you see news stations that say they want to interview an author or writer, reach out.

Become an expert on a topic. Write some articles, and publish videos on the topic. When a news agency needs an expert, let them seek you out. Politicians always trying to get interviewed sometimes have nothing to say, but it's about getting their name and message to the public. The more exposure the easier to get their jobs done.

8. Write an article

    We are all experts on something in our careers. What do you know so well that people seek you out? Once you know this, start putting ideas on paper.

        a)   Please write an article on the topic and find a publication to publish it to its users.

        b)   Article exposure is one of the keys to bringing customers to your website. As well as SEO (Search Engine Optimization systems) uses your website articles and posts to develop how high you appear in search engines.

9. Conferences

    Conferences are designed for a specific group of people. Presenting at one of these lets your target audience hear about your product and service. This presentation will reach people who are looking for new ideas. They are your specific market but getting listed as a presenter may require writing a good proposal or sponsoring some event with your hard-earned funds.

        a)   These presentations aren't about selling it is more about helping the attendees find solutions for their problems. If you can help them, this will be memorable and will stand out against the competition.

        b)   Design a presentation and write an abstract to submit to conferences. Use the knowledge you gained from your product research to discuss a current topic affecting the industry. Submit to as many as you can, the more you submit, the more chances you get for a presentation. We find that vendor presentations get fewer attendees but get lots of exposure. They are usually listed as specialized in the conference program.

c) If you are accepted, bring your product and talk about it at the end rather than the whole presentation.

d) Vendor Fairs – Most conferences have them. They work, but you need to design a presentation method to make you stand out. Your objective with a table at a vendor fair is to get people to sign up for your newsletter or collect their contact details.

This kind of conference exposure is what companies pay to attend or sponsor. It has been proven that an industry-specific conference has more opportunities for sales than any other avenue. Usually, because these employees do the work, they know what is needed. Management usually defers to them when a specific issue is discovered; when they have your contact details and are reaching out, you are almost guaranteed a sale.

10. Free talks

This is an easy way to get out about your product and service. Give free talks at senior centers, libraries, village halls, or anywhere that has an audience, and they are seeking someone to talk. These free events that may take time are the same way politicians get their ideas out. If politicians, financial experts, and town boards are speakers, they see this as valuable. Just remember to ensure this is your desired customer.

11. SWAG

I don't advise it for small businesses. With a tight budget, they don't get the results you want. Usually, people take extra small promotional items and don't utilize the product or service. SWAG does a good job when you are a large event and need to reinforce the customer to remember your company.

12. Creativity

This is crucial in getting any small business from a marketing perspective. One of the guys I interviewed a few years ago took his old van and put signs on both sides advertising his company. Unfortunately, he had a flat tire at a local mall in the parking lot. He had to leave the van there for a week until he could get the money to tow it. He got a few tickets, but the unexpected advertising was more than expected.

a) Stickers are the easiest way to be creative. You can make them with homemade kits or through countess internet-based sites. Showing up with some buttons as a giveaway can make your brand visible.

b) Wearing a t-shirt with your brand and with a funny comment. People will look toward your shirt and will have a mental image in their minds.

c) Be unique in a different way. Your focus is besides the two previous ideas, is how to get noticed by a large group to find out about your brand. People go to Street Fairs or outdoor markets to get noticed. A creative sign at a fair may make you stand out in the competition. One insurance carrier went to a street fair to hand out his flyer, which started a few conversations with potential customers.

13. Reddit

This is a platform where I have seen lots of success when people post regularly and answer questions. It reaches lots of people and marks your expertise in the industry. Cost little to nothing but is effective.

Summary:

People use these ideas to market, but remember that it's your audience, and you know it. Marketing is the art of getting noticed in your field. It's how you approach it that makes the difference.

What will the approach from the list above be practical for your product or service? Explain why you chose that one and how you will utilize it.

From an entrepreneur's perspective, we usually want the least costly marketing method to reach your niche's widest audience. How do you do that?

Research is an aspect that drives most things. The people who don't do research are kidding themselves by just jumping into work. I found that research in the industry, the related products/services, and the knowledge necessary for achievement work better than anyone just posting random junk.

Marketing is a challenge in today's society but by using these techniques and methods, you can set yourself apart from the countless market competitors.

$1200 and a Dream

Presentations

Giving a presentation is very easy. But it isn't as an entrepreneur; you have to think about what you would like to say; usually, you are working to convince someone to help you or be part of your business. We must ensure that we have any material prepared in a way that is crisp, clear, and persuasive all the same time.

How do you do that? That is the tricky part of any presentation, and it takes lots of practice to master this, but some methods work across all presentations that help us provide better insights to our audience.

The methods discussed can be implemented to help entrepreneurs focus on presentations and how to give them. By focusing on the Presentation, you will come across as clear and concise; delivers the main points first, then try to persuade somebody.

The necessary methods:

    a) Tell them your idea in a brief statement
    b) Describe the need for your service.
    c) Demonstrate the potential that is available by your idea
    d) Show due diligence that you did the research and know about the market
    e) Demonstrate that you or someone on the team has the contingency to solve the issue
    f) Ask them what you need from them, showing them how their participation can make a difference
    g) Summarize and thank them

I will go into detail on how to implement each of these. Please skim as needed to understand where you will gain the most knowledge from each idea.

a) Tell them your idea.

To tell them your idea, you need two parts. The Story and your vision. The Story is your business summary and the concept of the product or service you are offering.

Part 1.: To do you need to have a good story and something new and personal about why you feel you are doing this. The best entrepreneurs have a great story to tell of what impacted them to make them want to go into this field and get involved.

Example:
Here's my Story. I want to create a hands-on learning experience for my students at the local university where I work. I had seen an old, outdated machine shop 10 or 12 years ago at a high school. This space should be at the college level but interactive with technology. This area would be focused on empowering students to use technology and tools without bounds. It would expand on what they learned in the classroom to have them make strides we couldn't do with theory alone. My son was only in elementary school, but I knew that he was not alone and that he and others would need to be able to do hands-on experience to make a difference. I am uniquely positioned to implement this since I am working with university researchers with 3D printing technology that they feel will be the cornerstone of their classes and research. They need students to be able to use this technology to be successful in their endeavors. I pitched the idea to my supervisor and others to develop this hands-on experience in technology-driven innovative learning and maker space. We knew that was the future driving engineering education, so we launched it.

That was my passion. This story described why I launched the area and what I did, and it gave me the opening to keep the audience interested in our presentation. The presentation opening was what I needed to open any doors into additional conversations with stakeholders and partners. Focusing this in my career and my life has always been on the difference we can make in students' lives.

Education has to be all about the students, which needs to be remembered in C-suite, which focuses on profits.

The questions you need to ask yourself:

What's your Story?
The opening story is a short elevator pitch that will be your opening to the Presentation. Presentations are selling your idea to an audience; the story opening brings people together and gives them a connection to you that will give them the willingness to listen longer to hear the rest of the idea. You have to be both optimistic, emotional, and passionate all at the same time. Focus your Story on the difference you plan to make with your product/services. Writing a story is like telling anyone about your idea, just using your mission, vision, and customer work from the previous chapters put this together into a story.

We open with a story because it's persuasive, which makes you stand out among other presentations. It's a cheerful opening where people are waiting for financials, and it changes the audience's viewpoint on the Presentation to engage and interest.

Many tell you it's easiest to present in front of established investors because they know products and services better than new investors. No matter the case, we must find the right balance between sharing too much and too little.   It's best to have a maximum of one paragraph on why and the second is on how you will change the future. Only add details here on your idea; that is for the next section. You want to shrink it to a point so this can be your elevator pitch, and an elevator pitch is usually 45 seconds.

No matter how long or short, get to this point and tell them why they are here.   Think about a Disney story of Cinderella or Snow White. Can you summarize their Story in 45 seconds? Do the same for yours.

A great story differentiates between an all right and a fantastic presentation. Usually, this is the basis for why some investors get funded while others will not.

Write an outline of your story.

Part 2: Tell them your idea for your product or service.

What is your idea? For example, let us say your idea will disrupt the notebook market. You always want a student from K-12 never to have to buy new notebooks again. You are designing a new electronic laptop that is an app on your phone with an electronic feature to take your notes quickly and easily. You will never have to worry that you forgot your notebook again. The information will be stored in a shared cloud platform where parents and students can access it 24 hours a day—allowing the student and parents to collaborate on homework.

Your idea must be a summary without details but about the product/service. It gives the audience a quick overview of the idea. You may expand your idea to include enough so they understand the solution but only go into some technical details. Presentations sometimes focus too much on the product when they need to cover all aspects, including marketing, customer, and financials. This Presentation shows you have a solution for a problem in the marketplace, and your new company will solve the problem presented. It usually leaves numerous open questions, but it helps to get the interested person to focus. This is your objective.

b) Why is there a need for your idea?

The need is where you talk about what you have seen in the industry that needs to be improved. What can you deliver with this product/service that others can't? This is what makes you an entrepreneur. Your first message here is how you are different from others.

Your product has a specific thing, like an electronic app that only exists on phones but still feels like paper. This is called the Unique Selling Position (the statement that differentiates you from your competitors). Understanding how you stand out will help bolster your idea and target your market. In a presentation, you have developed something new by sharing this with the audience demonstrates.

c) Demonstrate the potential in the marketplace for your idea.

We want this section to focus on the industry. What is the size of the industry that you are trying to enter ? How many people are in the market, and what are the annual sales in the industry? This is where you want to have some basic research to figure this out. You are looking to have, in our example, know how many notebooks are being sold per year. How many pounds of paper are created? To do this, you would like to have public figures here to give the size and possible profits available.

- You would also like to include the number of students in the K-12 school marketplace in the United States. By doing this and knowing that an average notebook costs $2, you can make some profit assumptions.

- For example: If there are 200,000 students in the K-12 in the United States and they each purchase five notebooks a year. That means at $2 each; they spend $10 a year. Multiplying this by 200,000 gives you a $2,000,000 marketplace for laptops. If you want 4% of the market, that is $80,000. This demonstrates, in a simple example, the potential for profits in the market.

Some people will say this needs to include more, but this is a simplified example without real statistics to demonstrate how you develop the potential for your idea.

d) Show due diligence that you did the research and know about the market

This section is the research section of the idea. You want to look at what is happening in the marketplace for similar products. What are your competitors doing in the marketplace? How is your unique idea going to stand out? Where do you fit in vs others? This is where you have to demonstrate your product is better or has more potential in the marketplace you mentioned previously. Your customer discovery that you did earlier will help.

If you have tested the marketplace with similar products, this is where you would state this.

If you have no idea of how you will do it, be honest, but any details you can provide here are most worthwhile.

So many people need to learn the different market segments, but when you are selling your idea, showing you can and have done research is essential.

Research is done through Libraries, Online, and Databases, which we discussed earlier in the book. This information is what you want to showcase. One excellent idea is to purchase competitors' products and then showcase through video or live how your product solves the problem where there doesn't.

That type of research. First, what do you know about the industry?

Are there any competitors that sell the same product?

Are they making a profit?

e) Demonstrate that you have the knowledge or ability to solve the issue

There are times you stumble on a problem, and you need to find a solution. When you look to solve a problem its something, you were trying to solve on your desk or at your home recently. I just worked with a client who developed a solution for nurses to hold a needle a certain way for children who have felt pain with needles. This holder allowed the nurse to pinch the skin in a way that would generally deliver less pain and soreness to the affected area. Do you have unique knowledge of the situation that would solve this issue?

  a) This section of the Presentation focuses on the team and the value they bring to the Presentation. If you have a mechanic on the team, he knows that Kia cars break down for a specific reason, and he has worked with the team for a solution. Tell the audience.

b) Audience-specific knowledge is where you want to develop each person's biography. Each team member presenting should have a bio on a slide. This is your skills, knowledge, and expertise that you can share with the audience.

c) A bio should be at most 4-5 lines that include your name, education, work experience, expertise related to this project, and what makes you unique. (This last point concerns whether you have something that sets you apart from others. For example, You saved 100 lives by bringing paracord in need, and this donation helped nurses do their job more quickly. Did you create 5000 face shields to keep people safe during the pandemic.)

Write a practice Biography for yourself:

f) Demonstrate to them how their financial participation will make a difference:

This is the part of the Presentation most investors are waiting for in a presentation, demonstrating how they can participate in the idea. Please focus your efforts on the specifics of their investment, partnership, or collaboration in your business presentation. You only have one or two slides to demonstrate financials and show them the company's financials.

Financials to include in the Presentation: Estimated Projected revenue and costs

a) Costs generally include labor, acquisition, inventory, development of the produce/service, shipping, and marketing. The cost section is everything you would spend money on to help achieve your objective. We forget that there is a cost for everything, and the same is true when we are doing a new business. We need to do the hard work to document each of these costs. An easy way to see expenses is to look at a balance sheet online of a company. It will give you an outline.

b) Projected revenue is the amount you can earn by providing this product or service to the marketplace. This isn't profits which is the revenue minus the costs. This is just how much you will bring in from offering this product/service to potential buyers. This may involve some estimation where you are attempting to figure out how big of a market there is for this service and understand if you can get 2-5% of the market share. Make a conservative estimate for the investors.

c) I usually include a 3-year projection on all the revenue and costs. If I am unsure of the charges, ask someone with a good handle on any financials. Most accountants or financial planners can give you rough costs that you can include in any economic models for your Presentation.

Develop a 1-year cost projection for three personal doctors' offices. What would a doctor's office need to spend money on for 12 months?

g) *Finally, the Last Pitch:*

Be direct on where your audience could participate, either through an investment or working together in a joint business opportunity. By focusing on this, you are demonstrating there partnership can bring better results for both parties. Remember that you are doing this for your new business, but you must show how it will benefit the group you are persuading. If there is no benefit for them, they aren't going to want to get involved with your company.

The more details and information you can summarize in the above areas will help you convince anyone interested in investing or offering to spend their time to help your idea. Successful presentations are always about persuading someone to perform some action; mastering this takes time and practice.

There are tips that all Entrepreneurs need to know to deliver an excellent presentation. Enclosed are my tips to excel with sharing your ideas.

Guide to delivering an excellent presentation

Presentations are one of the most important aspects of a professional's position. A few tips helped me deliver many presentations to executives and students.
These tips have always given me lots of praise from people.

a) Don't read your PowerPoint slides. Too many people put everything on their PowerPoint slides and read them. Change the focus to be on you, not on your slides.

b) Use more pictures and graphics than text in your PowerPoint slides. Many people think that text is vital, but what you showcase is more critical if you know the material.

c) Practice, Practice, Practice. I can't say this enough. Practice what you are going to say. If you stand and say it aloud a few times to yourself, it will become smoother and more refined. The audience will be able to relate more to the content.

d) Please don't leave it to the last minute. I have seen too many people finishing their Presentations 30 minutes before they will give the talk. It will never come out the way you want if you do this.

e) Finish your presentation/speech at least four days in advance. I know this sounds crazy but finishing it a few days in advance. It allows you to practice and revise. The presentations on Shark Tank have been practiced at least 50 – 100 times.

f) Be yourself. Many people ask me if I should dress up for the Presentation, and my answer is that it depends on your audience. Everyone is dressed up if you are presenting to a group of bankers via zoom. Yes, please dress up. Business casual is perfect if you offer a group of students wearing pajamas. Be appropriate and business-like for the Presentation.

g) Know your audience. We often go into a room and need to know who will attend, and I look at the attendee list or ask the organizer for a list of presenters. Then do a quick LinkedIn search to ensure you know some background on each person.

h) Ask for what you want. When people present, they tell the material but don't ask or give a recommendation of what they are looking for from them. If you spend the time to ask them, this will set you apart from the presentations that forget.

i) Make them feel part of the idea. If they can become/embrace the picture, they will be more supportive of the Presentation. You need to ensure they have some buy-in. Usually, they will get on board with your idea if you can do this.

j) Nervousness happens. Don't worry about it. I have heard so many people say they have to perfect their Presentation, and it is not the perfect Presentation that convinces someone to support their idea. The ideal Presentation is the one who has the knowledge and can communicate the solution effectively.

Steps to become an Entrepreneur

We have covered much practical knowledge in the previous sections, but now it comes to the main question. What does it take to become an Entrepreneur? I have been asked this question countless times, and some simple steps are necessary to implement your idea.

This simple guide will focus your efforts on completing your startup.

a) Research the competitors in the marketplace to determine what products/services they offer that might be similar to yours.

b) Analyze your product/service to determine if there is anything you might need to change or modify. There are always improvements, but we are really focused on it being ready to go to market in the version it is now.

c) Reach out to Professors at Universities to see if they can give you feedback.

d) If you need help to launch it yourself, talk to manufacturers about building your product. This requires lots of putting your feet on the ground to find people who are good with their hands to make a prototype. Usually, maker spaces with 3D printers are an excellent place to develop a basic product/idea.

e) Your objective is to build a quick prototype. This is within a week or less. You need to demonstrate that something exists even if it is still a work in progress.

f) Talk to customers in your target market. Ask them if they like the idea or service. Gain feedback to determine if they would use it or not. In addition, ask carefully what type of price point they may pay for this product/service. This will give you more information on their thought process and your costs.

g) Revise, Revise, & Revise the idea. This is the stage where spending time implementing feedback you receive will make your idea better than your competitors.

h) Reach back out to customers and launch the product. Even giving away for free. This will give you invaluable insight into how desirable and useful the idea is. When it is free, sometimes you know if people will take it or even for free they leave it behind. If they leave it behind, they don't see a use for the product, or the offer could be better to be true. As an Entrepreneur, you need to understand what the customer thinks and why this will help them.

i) Revise as needed depending on the complimentary product/service giveaway response.

j) It's time to write your business plan to get investors or pitch your idea to others. This is where our chapters on networking & presentation skills are most important.

k) Sell them on your idea! Show how this idea is going to improve YYYZZZ's lives.

l) Now you are on your way to having your own company. Congratulations!

Good Luck.

We are always here to assist you as you move your idea forward.

Additional Resources

The author developed additional resources and advice where you can learn more information. Please follow and contact us on social media or email

Instagram: @icreatexps
TikTok: @icreatexp
YouTube: @icreatexp

If you find you have questions or corrections, please feel free to contact him at davidicreate@gmail.com

About the author

David Ecker is a Stony Brook University graduate who has worked at the university for 25+ years in technology management and leadership roles. In addition, is an entrepreneur with two business iCreate Experiences (icreatexp.com) and another to help others advance their careers and founded OurCareerCoaches.com to help professionals meet their life and career aspirations.

He focuses on innovation, the entrepreneurial spirit, and technology and believes hands-on learning is the future for success. David founded WolfieTank, a pitch competition for young entrepreneurs to present their ideas to a panel of Stony Brook alumni.

David made it possible for Stony Brook University to respond to the shortage of PPE during COVID by creating 3D-printed face shields for healthcare workers. He presented at TedX Stony Brook in 2013. His talk "When life throws you a curve ball" demonstrates how teachers can learn from students.

David holds a Master of Science in Technological Systems Management and a Bachelor of Science from Stony Brook University. In addition, he has an Advanced Graduate Certificate in Innovation & Entrepreneurship from Empire State College.

David lives on Long Island with his family.